SELENA GOMEZ

Making a Difference as a Singer and Actress

By Katie Kawa

KidHaven PUBLISHING

People Who Make a Difference

Published in 2024 by
KidHaven Publishing, an Imprint of Greenhaven Publishing, LLC
2544 Clinton St.
Buffalo, NY 14224

Designer: Deanna Paternostro
Editor: Katie Kawa

Photo credits: Cover Denis Makarenko/Shutterstock.com; p. 5 Andrea Raffin/Shutterstock.com; p. 7 s_bukley/Shutterstock.com; p. 9 Featureflash Photo Agency/Shutterstock.com; p. 11 Randy Miramontez/Shutterstock.com; p. 13 Tinseltown/Shutterstock.com; p. 15 Silvia Elizabeth Pangaro/Shutterstock.com; p. 17 Jacquelyn Martin/AP Photo; pp. 18, 20 DFree/Shutterstock.com; p. 21 T.Sumaetho/Shutterstock.com.

Library of Congress Cataloging-in-Publication Data

Names: Kawa, Katie, author.
Title: Selena Gomez : making a difference as a singer and actress / Katie Kawa.
Description: Buffalo, New York : KidHaven Publishing, [2024] | Series: People who make a difference | Includes bibliographical references and index.
Identifiers: LCCN 2023011283 | ISBN 9781534544208 (library binding) | ISBN 9781534544192 (paperback) | ISBN 9781534544215 (ebook)
Subjects: LCSH: Gomez, Selena, 1992–Juvenile literature. | Actors–United States–Biography–Juvenile literature. | Singers–United States–Biography–Juvenile literature. | LCGFT: Biographies.
Classification: LCC PN2287.G585 K39 2024 | DDC 791.4302/8092–dc23/eng/20230316
LC record available at https://lccn.loc.gov/2023011283

Printed in the United States of America

CONTENTS

A LIFE OF HIGHS AND LOWS

Life can be hard sometimes. Selena Gomez knows this very well. She's been famous since she was young and has had success as both a singer and an actress. However, she's also dealt with **serious** illnesses that have **affected** her body and her mind.

Selena didn't give up when things got hard. Instead, she's shared what she's gone through because she believes sharing your story is a powerful way to make a difference. Selena has **inspired** people through the stories she's told on TV and in the movies, but the true story of her life is even more inspiring.

In Her Words

"I think it's very brave to speak up about your own journey."

— Interview for the April 2022 Wondermind Newsletter

Selena Gomez is often in the spotlight, but she also knows what it's like to go through dark times. She's making a difference by helping others who are struggling feel understood and like they're not alone.

A YOUNG STAR

Selena got her start in the spotlight at a very young age. She was born on July 22, 1992, in Grand Prairie, Texas, and by 2002, she was working on the TV show *Barney & Friends*. Selena was a part of that show through 2004. Not long after that, she began working with the Disney Channel.

In 2007, Selena was offered the part of Alex Russo on the Disney Channel TV show *Wizards of Waverly Place*. She was a part of the show for five years, and it helped make her a big star.

In Her Words

"My mom was always teaching me not to be scared of life"

— *Selena Gomez: My Mind & Me*

Even when she was a young star, Selena was already doing what she could to help others. In 2009, she started working as a UNICEF ambassador. This means she **represents** UNICEF—a group that helps kids in need around the world.

MAKING MOVIES

While working on *Wizards of Waverly Place*, Selena also started making movies. She starred in the TV movies *Another Cinderella Story* in 2008 and *Princess Protection Program* in 2009. The next year, she made it to the big screen! She played Beezus in the movie *Ramona and Beezus*, which was based on a popular book for kids.

Selena's voice has also been in many different movies, including *Horton Hears a Who* in 2008 and *Dolittle* in 2020. She's also been the voice of Mavis in all the *Hotel Transylvania* movies.

In Her Words

"Hold on to your heart, try to be the best you can be, and be careful about who to trust, because you are who you surround yourself with."

— Interview with *Vanity Fair* magazine from February 2023

Selena has been a part of many kinds of movies—from love stories and funny movies to action movies and **animated** movies.

SELENA THE SINGER

Music is a big part of Selena's life too. She was part of a band called Selena Gomez & The Scene. Their first album, *Kiss & Tell*, came out in 2009. A year later, they came out with another album, *A Year Without Rain*. Their third album, *When the Sun Goes Down*, came out in 2011.

Selena then wanted to try making music on her own. In 2013, she put out her first solo album, *Stars Dance*. She followed that album with *Revival* in 2015 and *Rare* in 2020. The song "Lose You to Love Me" from *Rare* became Selena's biggest hit.

In Her Words

"It makes me proud I'm actually talking about things that matter."

— Interview with *Rolling Stone* magazine from November 2022

Selena became known for songs about learning how to love yourself—even when things are hard. These songs include "Who Says?" from *When the Sun Goes Down* and "Lose You to Love Me."

LIVING WITH LUPUS

Selena's star was rising, but at the same time, she was facing a serious health problem. She has lupus, which is a sickness that causes things to go wrong with the body's **immune system**. It can cause pain and fatigue, or tiredness. In some cases, it can also cause **kidney** problems. In 2017, Selena had a kidney transplant. One of her kidneys was taken out because it wasn't working correctly, and a healthy kidney from her friend was put into her body.

Selena has given a lot of money to help people dealing with lupus. She's also raised awareness about this sickness.

In Her Words

"It is important for people with lupus to look for help when needed and know you are not alone."

— Interview with
Lupus Research Alliance

Selena knows it's important to share what it's like to live with lupus to help others with it feel less alone. Her openness also helps people who don't have lupus better understand this sickness.

MENTAL HEALTH MATTERS

Selena has also been open about her **mental** health. In 2020, she shared that she has bipolar disorder. This can cause people to swing between periods of having too much energy and periods of feeling very down.

Selena wants to help get rid of the stigma, or negative view, surrounding mental illnesses. She's showing the world that having a mental illness doesn't have to stop someone from being successful. Selena also **encourages** her fans to take care of their own mental health. She tries to set a good example by sharing what she does to help herself, such as taking **social media** breaks.

In Her Words

"I wish more people talked about mental health when I was younger so I could have learned and understood what was going on with my own health earlier on."

— Note posted on the Rare Beauty website

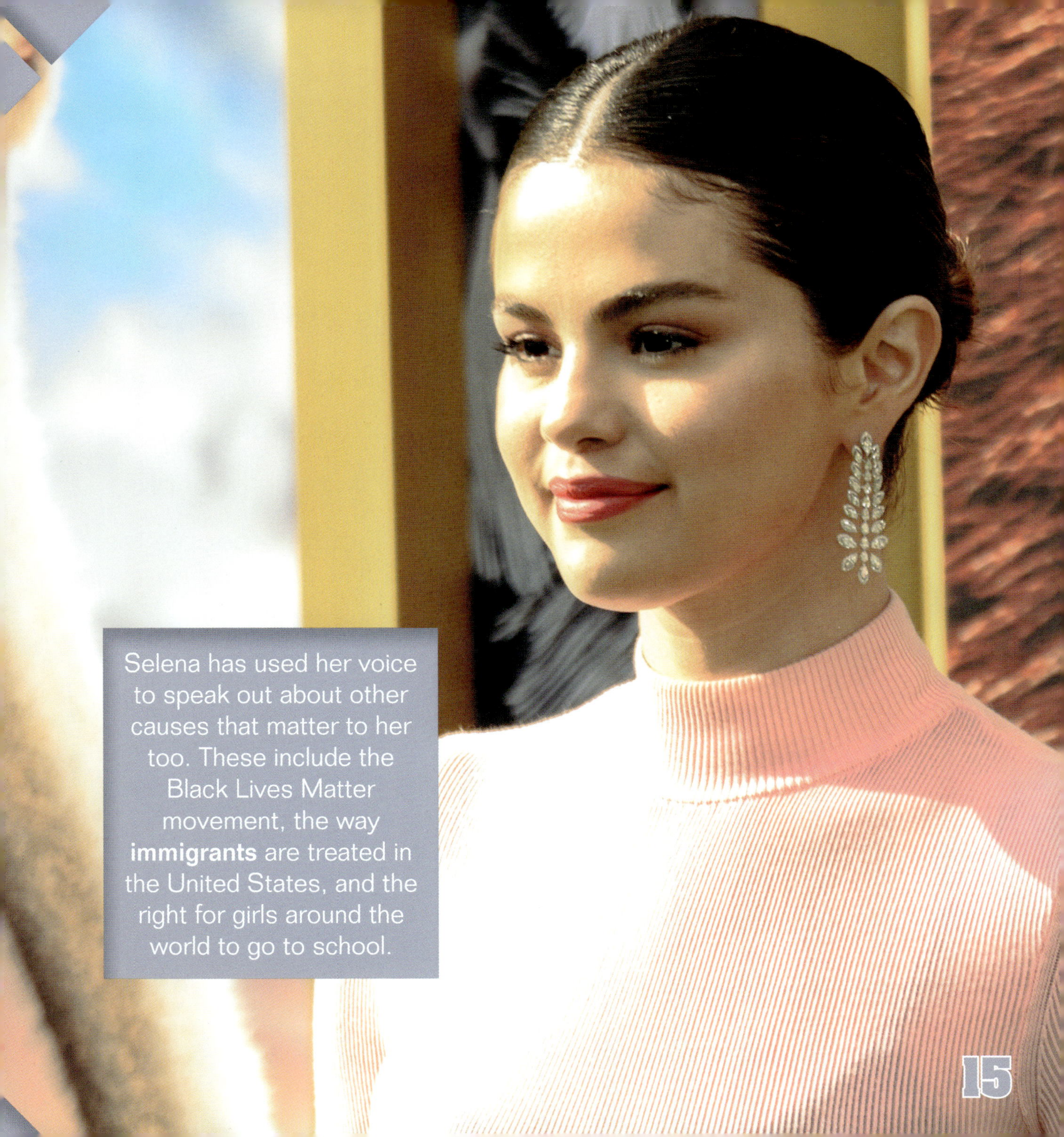

Selena has used her voice to speak out about other causes that matter to her too. These include the Black Lives Matter movement, the way **immigrants** are treated in the United States, and the right for girls around the world to go to school.

BEAUTIFUL INSIDE AND OUT

Selena has said she wants to help people, especially young women, show off what makes them unique, or special. One of the ways she's doing this is through her beauty brand, Rare Beauty. She launched, or started, this brand in 2020 with the goal of creating makeup and other beauty products that help people feel comfortable in their own skin.

When someone buys a Rare Beauty product, some of the money goes toward the Rare Impact Fund. This provides money for mental health **resources** for young people in places such as schools.

In Her Words

"I hope by sharing my own story and using my brand … to talk about and connect more people to resources that support their mental health, I can encourage others to get the help they need and bring more mental health services to educational settings."

— Note posted on the Rare Beauty website

Selena visited the White House in 2022
to talk about mental health with other important people,
including Dr. Jill Biden, the First Lady of the United States.

INSIDE HER MIND

Selena's belief that it should be easier to find mental health resources led to the creation of a **platform** called Wondermind in 2022. The Wondermind website has tips and stories to help people take care of their mental health and to better understand mental illnesses. Selena is one of the founders of Wondermind, and her mother is one too!

Later in 2022, Selena gave people an even closer look at her mental health journey in the movie *Selena Gomez: My Mind & Me*. Many people were inspired by this movie to talk more openly about their own mental health struggles.

In Her Words

"At the end of the day, I do want to be impactful [make a difference] in some way. And if that's by sharing a part of myself that isn't … pretty and put together, there are hopefully people that can look at that and think, Oh, maybe I feel this way, or, I didn't know that you could get this kind of help."

— Interview with *Vogue* magazine from November 2022

The Life of Selena Gomez

1992
Selena Gomez is born in Grand Prairie, Texas.

2002–2004
Selena is part of the TV show *Barney & Friends*.

2007
Selena begins playing Alex Russo on *Wizards of Waverly Place*.

2008
Selena stars in *Another Cinderella Story*, and her voice is used in *Horton Hears a Who*.

2009
Selena stars in *Princess Protection Program*, releases *Kiss & Tell* with The Scene, and becomes an ambassador for UNICEF.

2010
Selena plays Beezus in *Ramona and Beezus*, and Selena Gomez & The Scene release *A Year Without Rain*.

2011
When the Sun Goes Down is released.

2013
Selena puts out her first solo album, *Stars Dance*.

2015
Selena releases the album *Revival*.

2017
Selena has a kidney transplant because of problems caused by lupus.

2020
Selena releases the album *Rare*, starts the brand Rare Beauty, and tells the public she has bipolar disorder.

2021
Selena begins acting on the TV show *Only Murders in the Building*.

2022
Selena helps create the Wondermind website, and *Selena Gomez: My Mind & Me* comes out.

Selena Gomez has been in the spotlight since she was a little kid, and now she's using that spotlight to call attention to issues that mean a lot to her.

WHAT'S NEXT?

Selena knows she can raise awareness about issues such as mental illness and lupus because she's one of the most famous women in show business. Her fame reached new heights in 2021, when she first appeared on the TV show *Only Murders in the Building*. The show has become a huge hit, and Selena is a big part of its success.

Selena has said she wants to keep making music, movies, and TV shows, but what she really wants to do is keep helping people. She believes making a difference in someone's life is more important than being famous.

In Her Words

"I'd rather be remembered for my heart than anything else."

— Interview with *Vanity Fair* magazine from February 2023

Be Like Selena Gomez!

Raise money for groups that help people with lupus or another serious illness.

Take care of your mental health by doing things that make you feel happy or calm, such as writing in a journal, moving your body, or talking to a friend.

Help others feel less alone by listening to them.

If you know someone who's having a hard time with their mental health, support them, and tell a trusted adult.

Raise money for groups that help people with their mental health.

If you're having a hard time with your mental health, tell a trusted adult about what you're feeling.

Learn more about mental health and mental illnesses.

Remind your friends and family members that it's OK to talk openly about your feelings and your mental health.

Talk openly with others about issues that are important to you.

Selena Gomez has said she believes life is all about how we connect with others. If you want to be more like her, you can start by being kind and caring.

GLOSSARY

affect: To produce an effect on something.

animated: Made using a series of drawings, pictures, or computer-created images that are shown quickly one after another.

encourage: To make someone more likely to do something.

immigrant: A person who comes to a country to live there.

immune system: The group of body parts and cells that work together to keep the body safe from things that might harm it or make it sick.

inspire: To move someone to do something great.

kidney: Either of a pair of oval body parts located in back part of the body near the spine that give off waste products in the form of urine.

mental: Relating to the mind.

platform: An application or website that serves as a base from which a service is provided.

represent: To act officially or stand for someone or something.

resource: Something that can be used.

serious: Causing worry or harm.

social media: A collection of websites and applications, or apps, that allow users to interact with each other and create online communities.

FOR MORE INFORMATION

WEBSITES

Rare Beauty's Self Care and Mental Health Blog

www.rarebeauty.com/blogs/news

This part of the Rare Beauty website allows visitors to learn more about mental illnesses, ways to care for their own mental health, and how to support others.

Selena Gomez

www.selenagomez.com/

Selena Gomez's official website features facts about her life and work, as well as links to learn more about Rare Beauty and the Rare Impact Fund.

BOOKS

Andral, Dolores. *What You Never Knew About Selena Gomez.* North Mankato, MN: Capstone Press, 2023.

Audra, Janari. *Mental Health in Our World.* New York, NY: PowerKids Press, 2022.

Neuenfeldt, Elizabeth. *Selena Gomez: Mental Health Advocate.* Minnetonka, MN: Bellwether Media, 2022.

INDEX